Contents

Phonics Centers
Level A

What's Great About This Book

Centers are a wonderful, fun way for students to practice important skills. The 13 centers in this book are self-contained and portable. Students may work at a table or even on the floor. Once you've made the centers, they're ready to use at any time.

Everything You Need

- Teacher direction page

    How to make the center

    Description of student task

- Full-color materials needed for the center
- Reproducible student activity sheets

Using the Center

The centers are intended for skill practice, not to introduce skills. It is important to model the use of each center before students do the task independently.

Questions to Consider

- Will students select a center, or will you assign one?
- Will there be a specific block of time for centers, or will the centers be used throughout the day?
- Where will you place the centers for easy access by students?
- What procedure will students use when they need help with the center tasks?
- Where will students store completed work?
- How will you track the tasks and centers completed by each student?

Making an Envelope Center

Materials

- 9" x 12" (23 x 30.5 cm) large envelopes
- scissors
- marking pens
- glue or two-sided tape

Steps to Follow

1. Remove and laminate the center cover page. Glue or tape it to the front of the envelope.

2. Remove and laminate the student directions page. Glue or tape it to the back of the envelope.

3. Remove, laminate, and cut apart the manipulatives (sorting mats, task cards, pockets, etc.) and place them in the envelope.

4. Reproduce copies of the student activity sheet and place them in the envelope.

Note: If a center contains small pieces such as letter cards, place them in a smaller envelope within the larger envelope.

Center Cover

Student Directions

Student Activity Sheet

Task Cards

Sorting Pocket

If the center contains a sorting pocket, score lightly with scissors on the fold line. Fold up and staple the pocket on each side.

Puppy Match

Skill: Visual Discrimination

Preparing the Center

1. Prepare an envelope following the directions on page 3.
    Cover—page 5
    Student Directions—page 7
    Task Cards—pages 9 and 11
2. Reproduce a supply of the student activity sheet on page 13.
3. Place all center materials in the envelope.

Using the Center

In a Small Group

A student chooses a dog, describes the color or pattern on its bandana, and then lays it faceup on a flat surface. The next student chooses another dog, describes its bandana, and lays it down. If a dog matches a dog already played, it is piled on top of the matching dog.

Independently

The student matches cards with dogs that have the same kind of bandana.

The student completes the activity sheet by drawing lines to matching dogs.

Self-Checking Key

Students turn the cards over to make sure the back of the cards match.

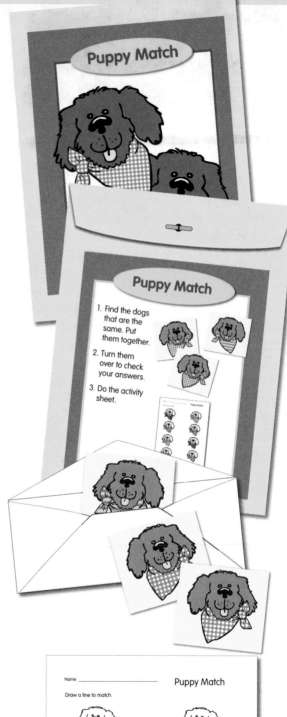

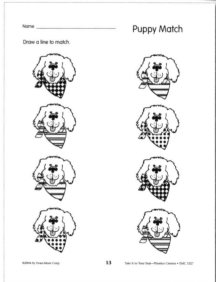

Puppy Match

Take It to Your Seat—Phonics Centers • EMC 3327

6

Puppy Match

1. Find the dogs that are the same. Put them together.

2. Turn them over to check your answers.

3. Do the activity sheet.

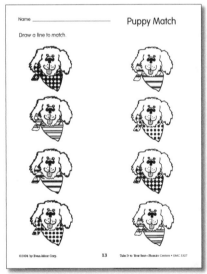

Skill: Visual Discrimination

8

Name _____

Draw a line to match.

Find the Pairs

Skill: Visual Discrimination

Preparing the Center

1. Prepare an envelope following the directions on page 3.
   Cover—page 15
   Student Directions—page 17
   Task Cards—pages 19–25
2. Reproduce a supply of the student activity sheet on page 27.
3. Place all center materials in the envelope.

Using the Center

In a Small Group

A student chooses a card, looks at the letter, and then lays it faceup on a flat surface. The next student chooses another card, looks at it, and lays it down. If a card matches a card already on the table, it is piled on top of the matching card.

Independently

The student sorts the letter cards into pairs.

The student colors letters on the activity sheet to show that they are the same.

Self-Checking Key

Matching cards have the same design on the back.

Find the Pairs

16

Find the Pairs

1. Find the mittens that are the same.

2. Put them together.

3. Turn them over to see if the designs match.

4. Do the activity sheet.

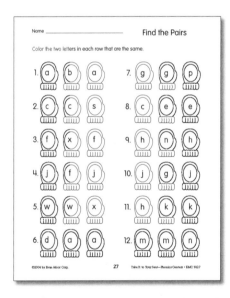

Skill: Visual Discrimination

18

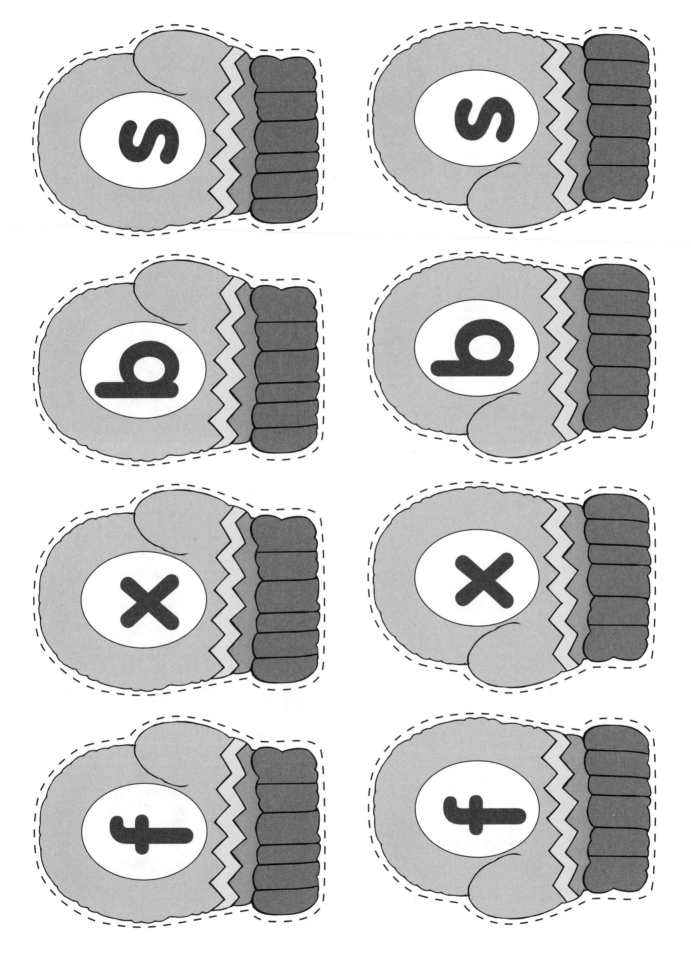

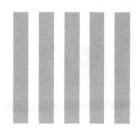

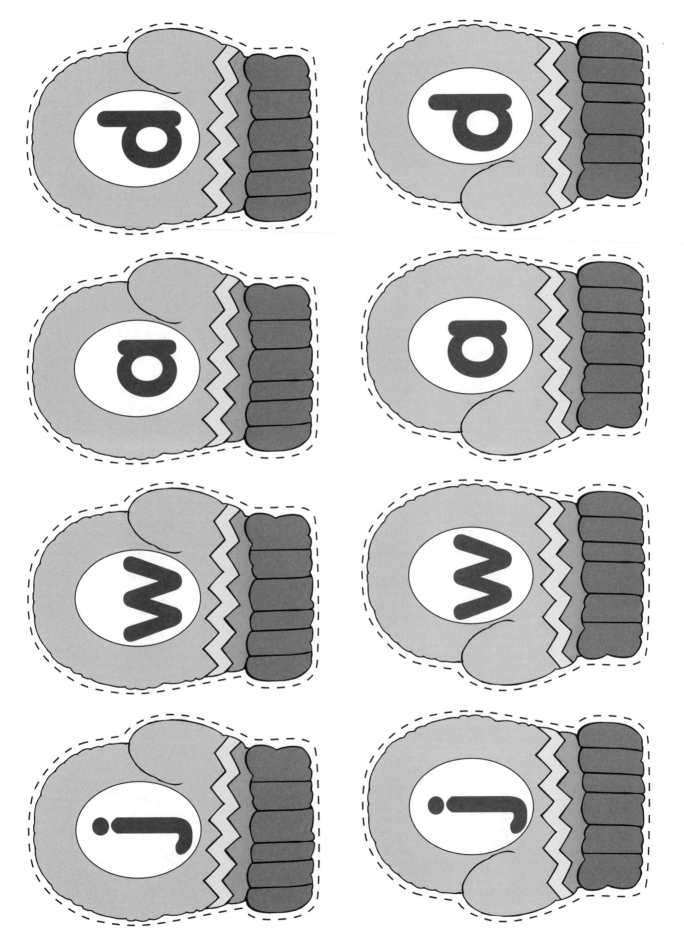

©2004 by Evan-Moor Corp.
Take It to Your Seat—
Phonics Centers
EMC 3327

©2004 by Evan-Moor Corp.
Take It to Your Seat—
Phonics Centers
EMC 3327

©2004 by Evan-Moor Corp.
Take It to Your Seat—
Phonics Centers
EMC 3327

©2004 by Evan-Moor Corp.
Take It to Your Seat—
Phonics Centers
EMC 3327

©2004 by Evan-Moor Corp.
Take It to Your Seat—
Phonics Centers
EMC 3327

©2004 by Evan-Moor Corp.
Take It to Your Seat—
Phonics Centers
EMC 3327

©2004 by Evan-Moor Corp.
Take It to Your Seat—
Phonics Centers
EMC 3327

©2004 by Evan-Moor Corp.
Take It to Your Seat—
Phonics Centers
EMC 3327

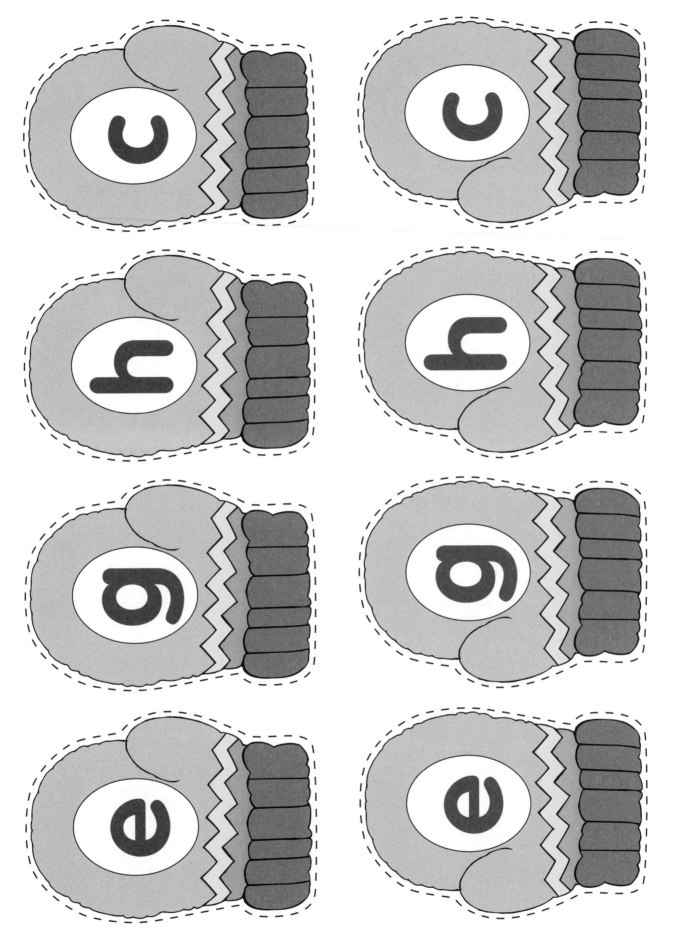

23

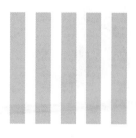

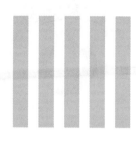

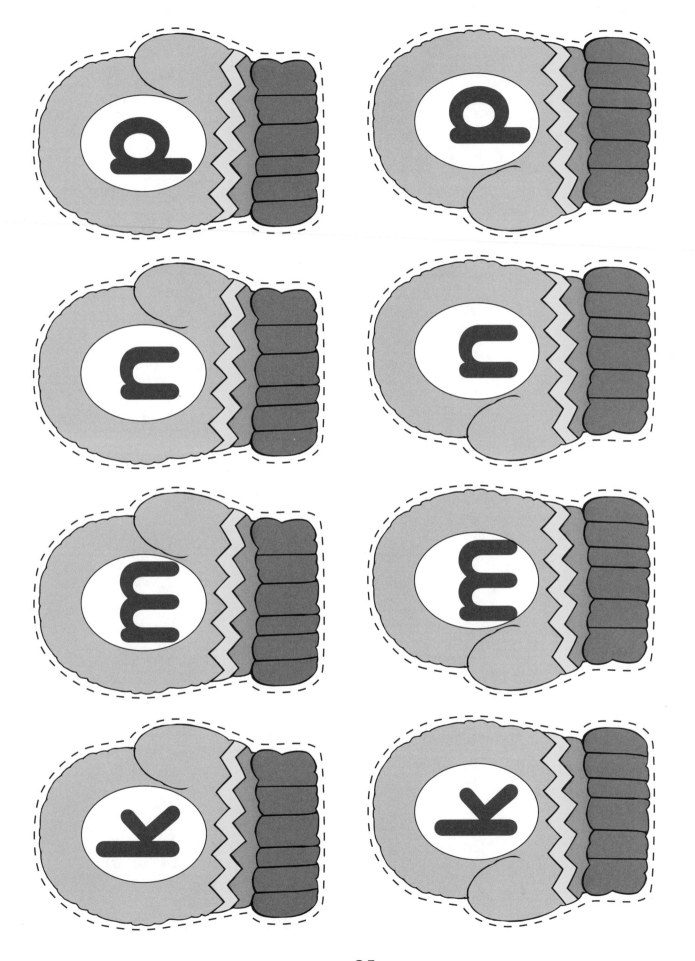

Find the Pairs

Color the two letters in each row that are the same.

1.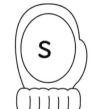

2.

3.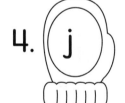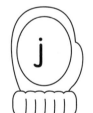

4.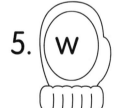

5.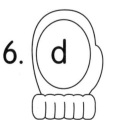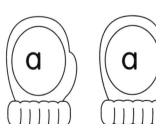

6.

7.

8.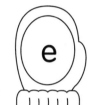

9.

10.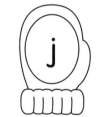

11.

12.

Three of a Kind

Skill: Visual Discrimination

Preparing the Center

1. Prepare an envelope following the directions on page 3.
   - Cover—page 29
   - Student Directions—page 31
   - Task Cards—strips on pages 33–37
     - cards on page 39
2. Reproduce a supply of the student activity sheet on page 41.
3. Place all center materials in the envelope.

Using the Center

In a Small Group

A student chooses a strip, identifies which object or letter is different, and then lays it faceup on a flat surface. Next, the student finds a small card to make all three objects on the strip the same. The card is laid on top of the object that is different.

The next student chooses a strip and repeats the process. Continue until all strips have been completed.

Independently

The student uses the small cards to make each strip show the same three objects or letters.

Then the student completes the activity sheet by circling "three of a kind" in each row.

Self-Checking Key

The object and letter strips have the correct design on the back.

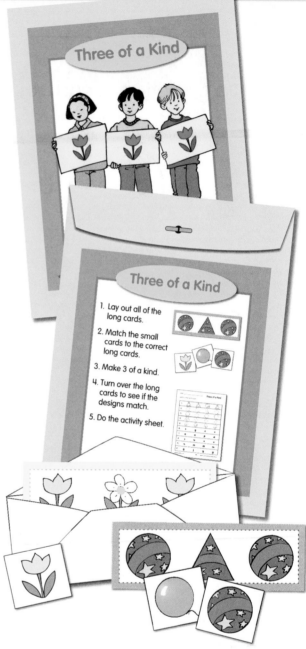

Three of a Kind

30

Three of a Kind

1. Lay out all of the long cards.

2. Match the small cards to the correct long cards.

3. Make 3 of a kind.

4. Turn over the long cards to see if the designs match.

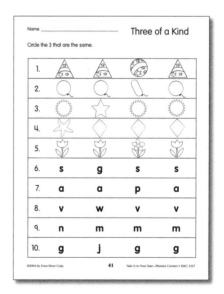

5. Do the activity sheet.

Skill: Visual Discrimination

31 Take It to Your Seat—Phonics Centers • EMC 3327

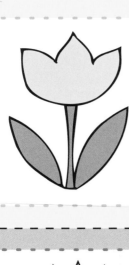

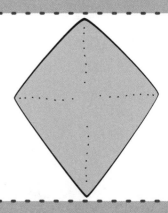

34

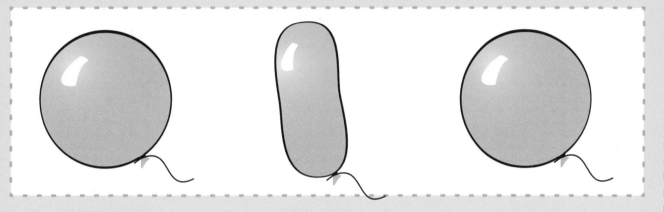

g   g   b

s   c   s

35

g g g

s s s

a p p

w v w

m n n

j g j

p p p

w w w

n n n

j j j

Name _____

Circle the 3 that are the same.

1.				
2.				
3.				
4.				
5.				
6.	s	g	s	s
7.	a	a	p	a
8.	v	w	v	v
9.	n	m	m	m
10.	g	j	g	g

Take It to Your Seat—Phonics Centers • EMC 3327

Rhyming Pairs

Skill: Rhyming Words

Preparing the Center

1. Prepare an envelope following the directions on page 3.
   - Cover—page 43
   - Student Directions—page 45
   - Task Cards—pages 47–51
2. Reproduce a supply of the student activity sheet on page 53.
3. Place all center materials in the envelope.

Using the Center

In a Small Group

Students take turns choosing a picture card and naming the object. When a picture is named that forms a rhyming pair, the cards are fit together.

Independently

The student forms rhyming puzzle pairs from the picture cards.

Students then match pairs on the activity sheet.

Self-Checking Key

Puzzle pieces of rhyming pairs fit together.

Rhyming Pairs

44

Rhyming Pairs

1. Choose a card. Name the picture.

2. Find another card that rhymes.

3. Match all the rhyming pairs.

4. Do the activity sheet.

Skill: Rhyming Words

46

Name _____

Rhyming Pairs

Draw a line to show the rhyme.

Rhyme Squares

Skill: Rhyming Words

Preparing the Center

1. Prepare an envelope following the directions on page 3.
   Cover—page 55
   Student Directions—page 57
   Task Cards—pages 59–63
2. Reproduce a supply of the student activity sheet on page 65.
3. Place all center materials in the envelope.

Using the Center

In a Small Group

Students spread out the cards faceup on a flat surface. Students then take turns choosing and naming a picture, listening for rhyming words. Pictures that rhyme are grouped together to complete six four-picture squares.

Independently

The student forms six sets of rhyming picture squares.

Then the student demonstrates proficiency with rhyming words by cutting and pasting to make two rhyming squares on the activity sheet.

Self-Checking Key

Turn over the four pieces of each set. When grouped correctly, the puzzle pieces can be rearranged to make a picture of an object that rhymes with the four smaller pictures.

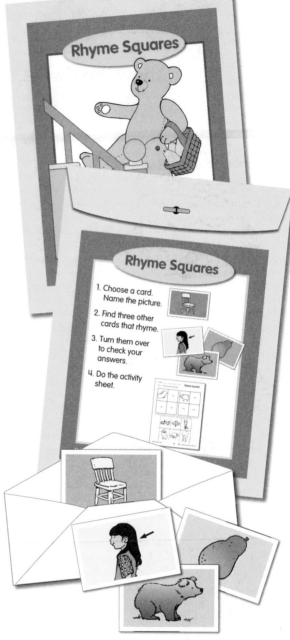

Rhyme Squares

56

Rhyme Squares

1. Choose a card. Name the picture.

2. Find three other cards that rhyme.

3. Turn them over to check your answers.

4. Do the activity sheet.

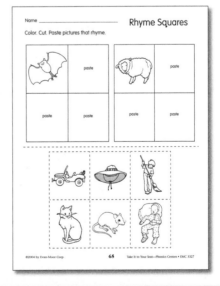

Skill: Rhyming Words

58

 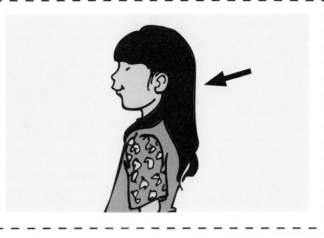

 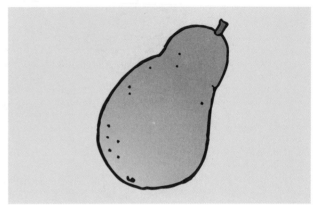

 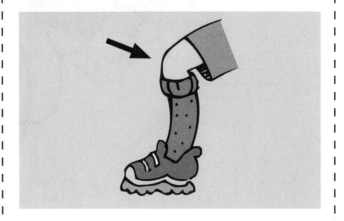

Take It to Your Seat—Phonics Centers • EMC 3327

Take It to Your Seat—Phonics Centers • EMC 3327

61

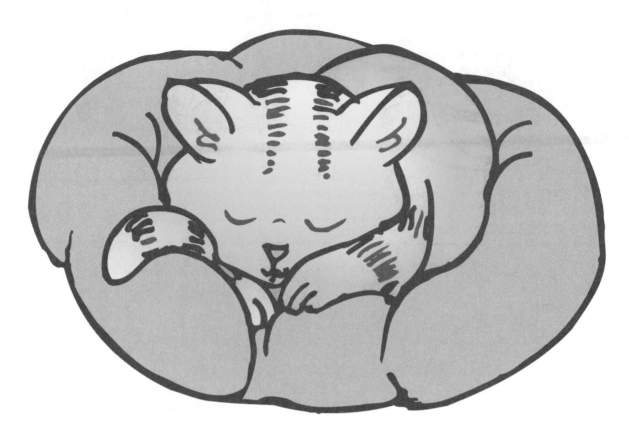

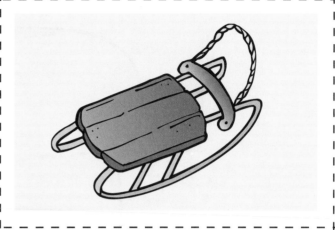

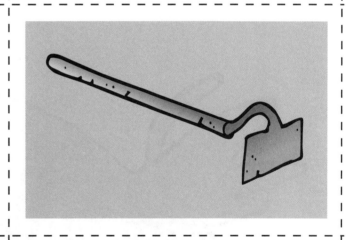

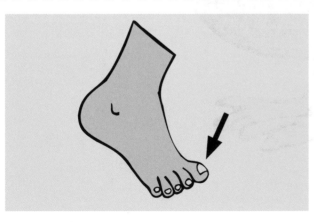

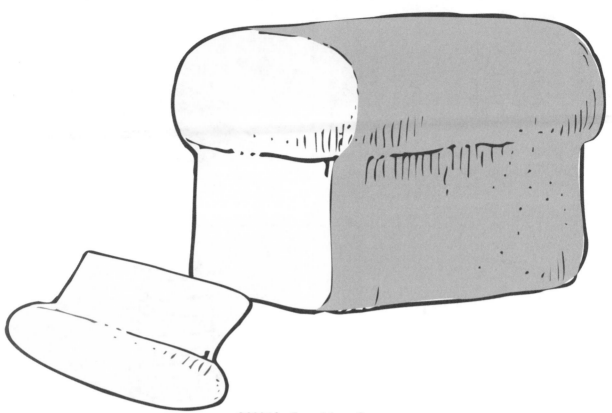

Name _____

Rhyme Squares

Color. Cut. Paste pictures that rhyme.

	paste
paste	paste

	paste
paste	paste

Alike– Not Alike

Skill: Identifying Like Letters

Preparing the Center

1. Prepare an envelope following the directions on page 3.
   - Cover—page 67
   - Student Directions—page 69
   - Sorting Mats—pages 71 and 73
   - Task Cards—page 75
2. Reproduce a supply of the student activity sheet on page 77.
3. Place all center materials in the envelope.

Using the Center

In a Small Group

Place the cards in a paper bag. Place the sorting mats faceup on a table. A student reaches into the bag and removes a card. The group looks at the letters on the card and decides if the two letters are alike or not alike. They then place the card on the correct sorting mat. The students work together to sort all of the cards remaining in the bag.

Independently

The student sorts the cards into alike and not alike sets on the sorting mats.

Then the student completes the activity sheet, marking the smiling face if the two letters are alike and the frown if they are not alike.

Self-Checking Key

Alike cards have a smiling clown face on the back. Cards that are not alike have a frowning clown face on the back.

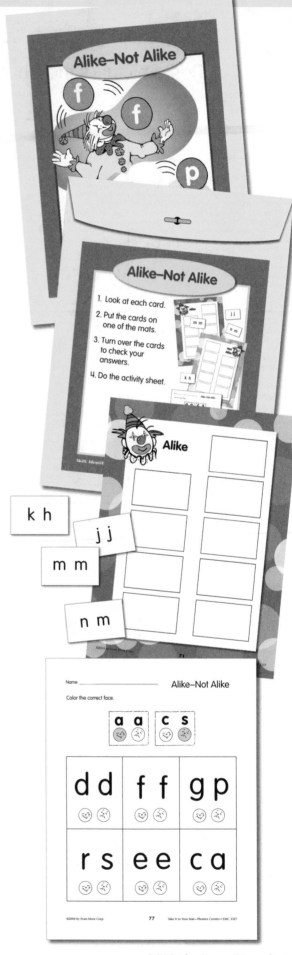

Alike–Not Alike

68

Alike–Not Alike

1. Look at each card.

2. Put the cards on one of the mats.

3. Turn over the cards to check your answers.

4. Do the activity sheet.

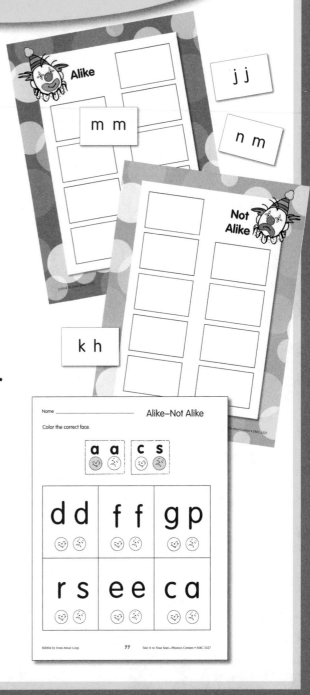

Skill: Identifying Like Letters

Alike

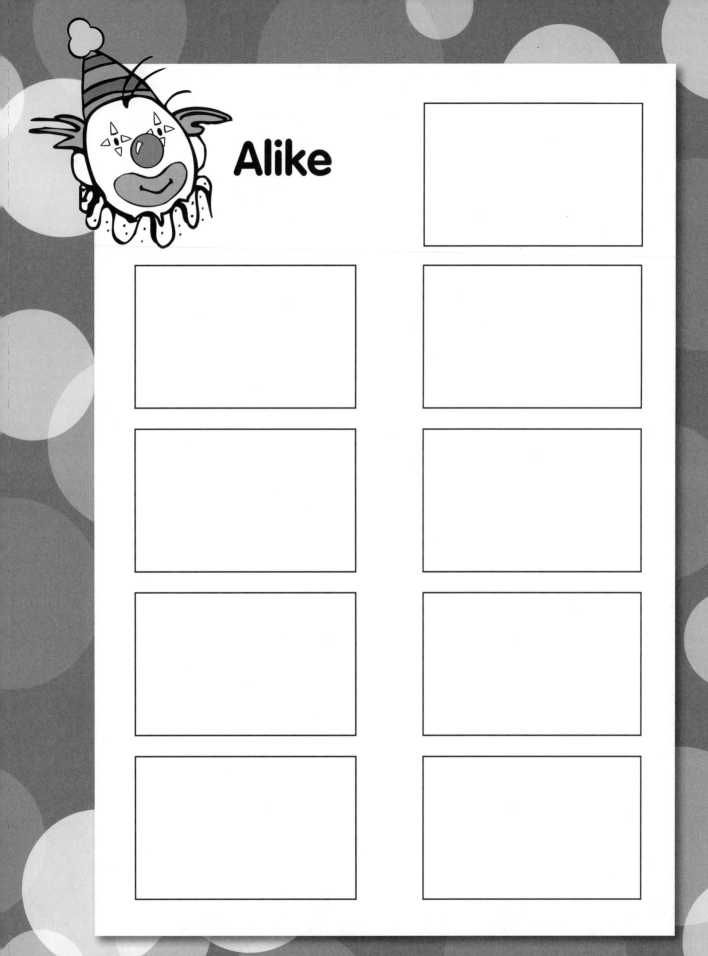

72

Not Alike

74

c c	b b	j j
z z	m m	f f
w w	g g	k k
s c	g p	b d
n m	l t	z w
k h	r s	v u

Take It to Your Seat—Phonics Centers • EMC 3327

Color the correct face.

d d	f f	g p
r s	e e	c a

Match It Up

Skill: Recognizing Upper- and Lowercase Letters

Preparing the Center

1. Prepare an envelope following the directions on page 3.
   - Cover—page 79
   - Student Directions—page 81
   - Task Cards—pages 83–91
2. Reproduce a supply of the student activity sheet on page 93. (Use the handwriting style appropriate for your class.)
3. Place all center materials in the envelope.

Using the Center

In a Small Group

Place the cards in a paper bag. Students reach into the bag and remove ladybug sections. The group reads the letter on each section. They work together to match upper- and lowercase letters to form whole ladybugs.

Independently

Using the ladybug sections, the student matches the upper- and lowercase letters.

Then the student traces the letters on the student activity sheet.

Self-Checking Key

Matching cards have the same colored design on the back.

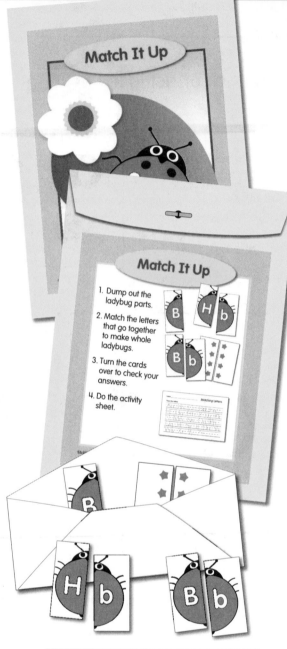

78

Match It Up

79

80

Match It Up

1. Dump out the ladybug parts.

2. Match the letters that go together to make whole ladybugs.

3. Turn over the cards to check your answers.

4. Do the activity sheet.

Name _____   Matching Letters

Trace the letters.

Aa Bb Cc Dd Ee
Ff Gg Hh Ii Jj Kk
Ll Mm Nn Oo Pp
Qq Rr Ss Tt Uu Vv
Ww Xx Yy Zz

Skill: Recognizing Upper- and Lowercase Letters

Match It Up!

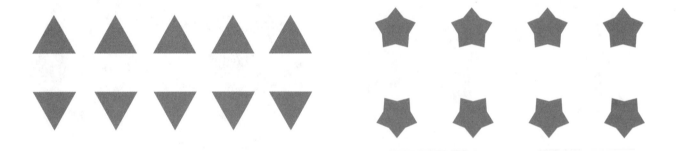

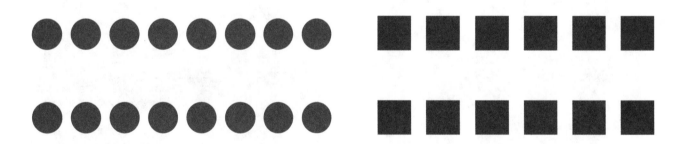

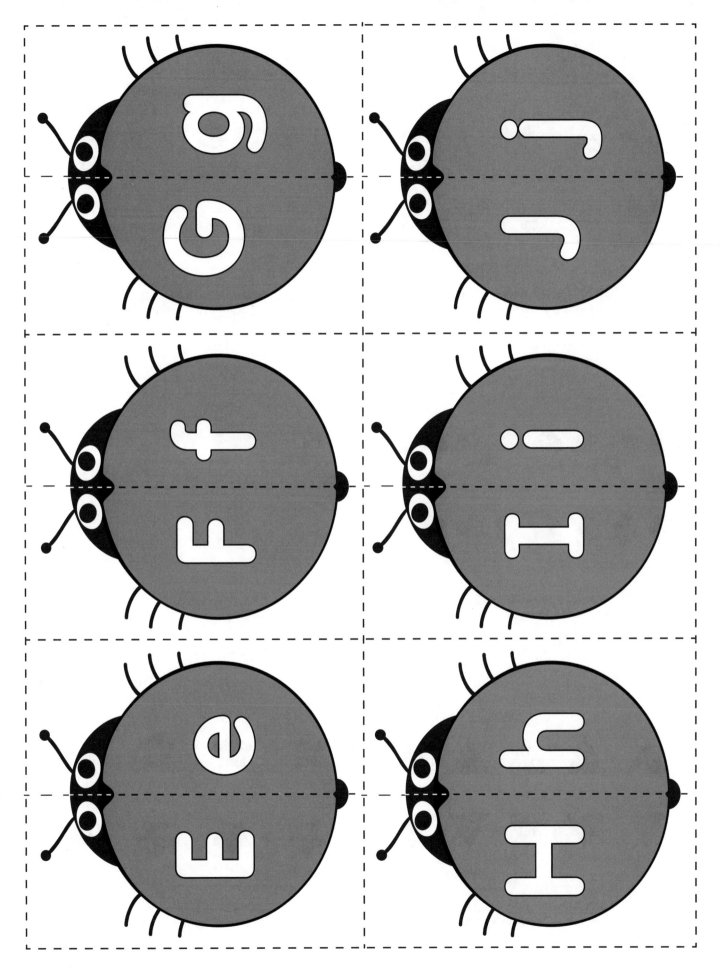

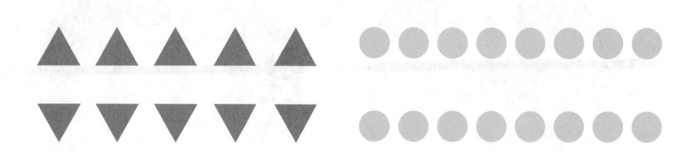

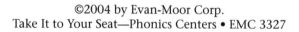

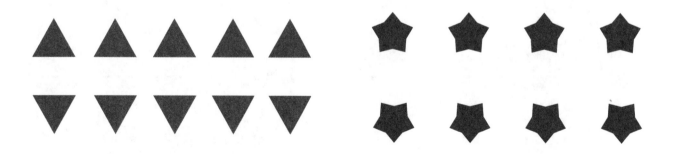

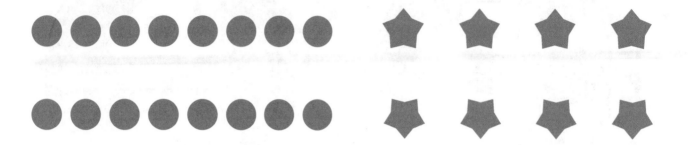

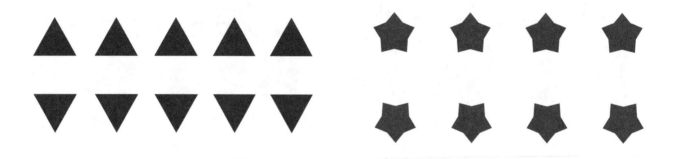

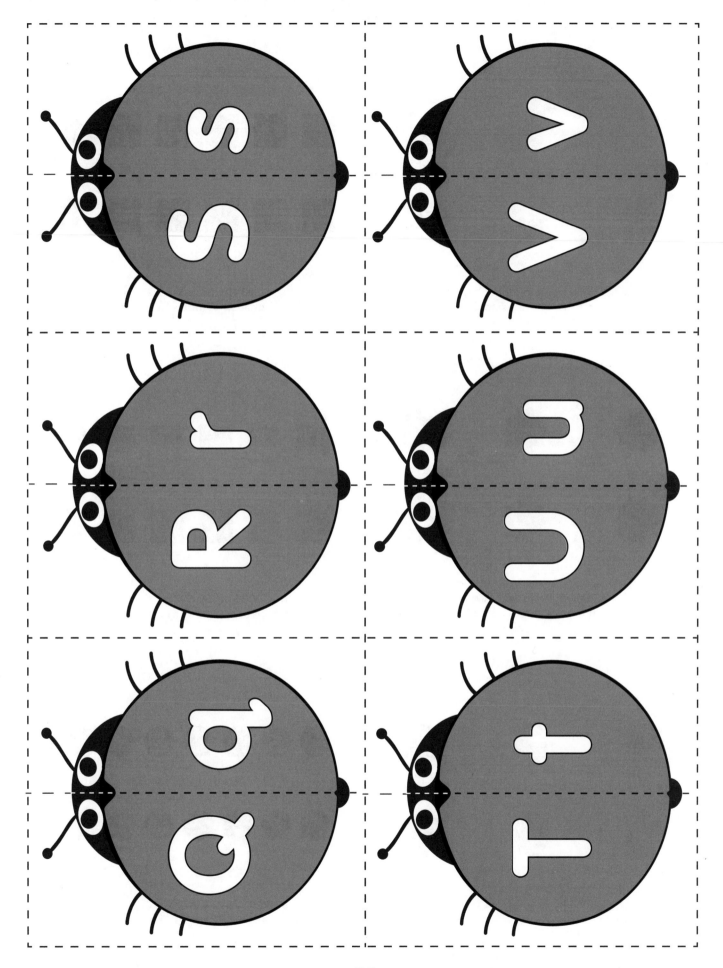

89

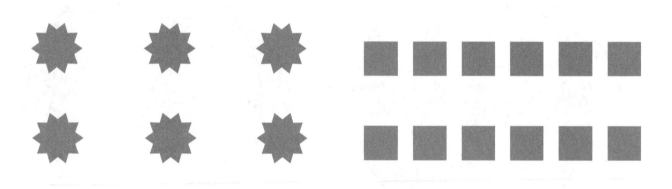

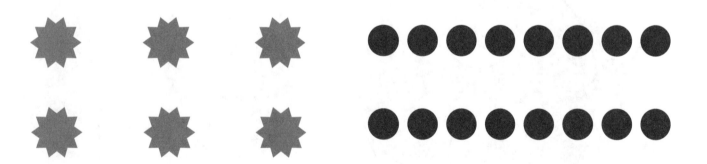

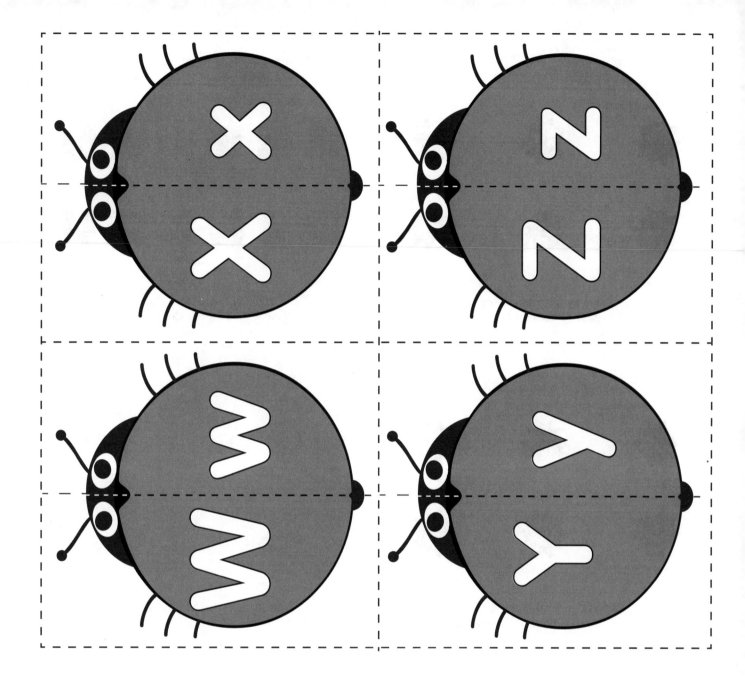

91

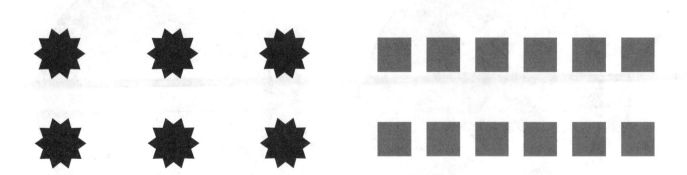

Name _____

Matching Letters

Trace the letters.

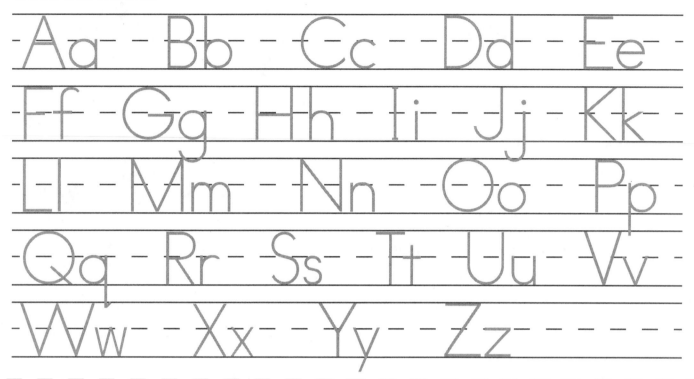

Aa Bb Cc Dd Ee
Ff Gg Hh Ii Jj Kk
Ll Mm Nn Oo Pp
Qq Rr Ss Tt Uu Vv
Ww Xx Yy Zz

Name _____

Matching Letters

Trace the letters.

Aa Bb Cc Dd Ee
Ff Gg Hh Ii Jj Kk
Ll Mm Nn Oo Pp
Qq Rr Ss Tt Uu Vv
Ww Xx Yy Zz

Beginning Sounds

Skill: Listening for Initial Consonant Sounds: *b, f, h, l, m, p, s, w*

Preparing the Center

1. Prepare an envelope following the directions on page 3.
    Cover—page 95
    Student Directions—page 97
    Sorting Mats—pages 99 and 101
    Picture Cards—pages 103–107
2. Reproduce a supply of the student activity sheet on page 109.
3. Place all center materials in the envelope.

Using the Center

In a Small Group
Lay the picture cards faceup on a flat surface. Hold up a sorting mat showing a letter and a picture beginning with that sound. Students find picture cards whose names begin with the same sound. Students name each of the pictures and listen for the sound of the letter.

Independently
The student lays the sorting mats on a flat surface. The student selects a picture card and names the picture. Then the student puts the card on the sorting mat that stands for the sound that is heard at the beginning of the word.

The student draws one picture for each letter on the activity sheet.

Self-Checking Key
Turn over each set of picture cards. The letter on the back of each card should match the letter on the sorting mat.

Beginning Sounds

96

Beginning Sounds

1. Say the name of each picture. Listen for the beginning sound.

2. Put each card on the mat that shows the letter for the beginning sound.

3. Turn over the cards to check your answers.

4. Do the activity sheet.

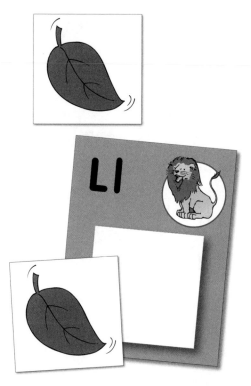

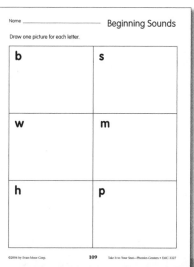

Skill: Listening for Initial Consonants: *b, f, h, l, m, p, s, w*

98

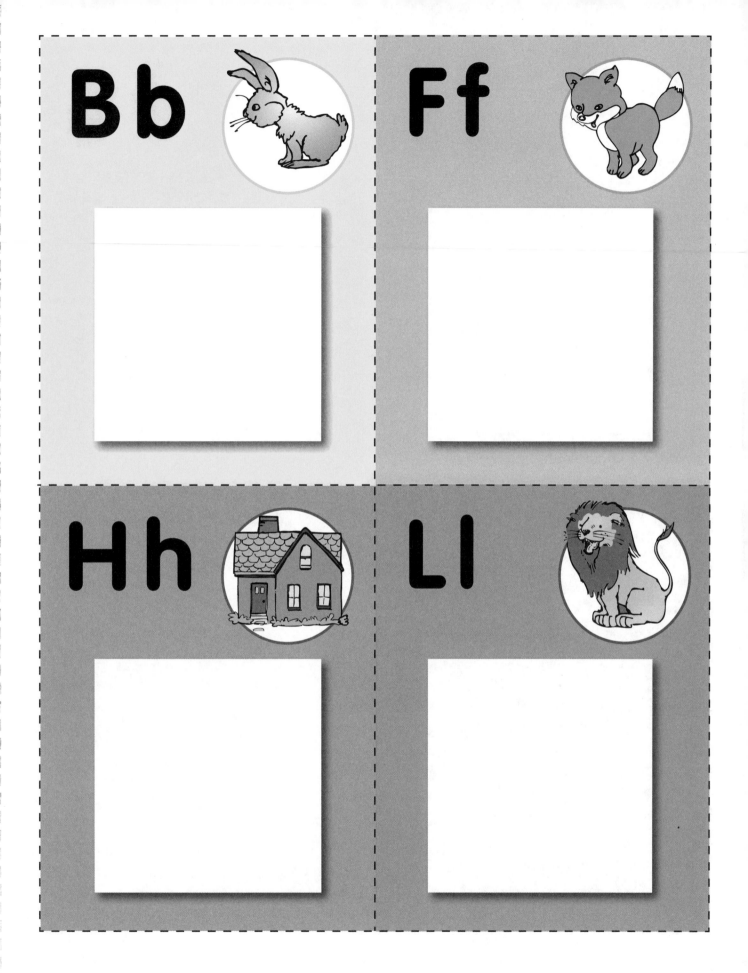

B b

F f

H h

L l

M m

P p

S s 6

W w

©2004 by Evan-Moor Corp.
Take It to Your Seat—Phonics Centers
EMC 3327

©2004 by Evan-Moor Corp.
Take It to Your Seat—Phonics Centers
EMC 3327

©2004 by Evan-Moor Corp.
Take It to Your Seat—Phonics Centers
EMC 3327

©2004 by Evan-Moor Corp.
Take It to Your Seat—Phonics Centers
EMC 3327

Hh

Ss

Bb

Hh

Ss

Bb

Hh

Ss

Bb

Hh

Ss

Bb

Ll

Mm

Ww

Ll

Mm

Ww

Ll

Mm

Ww

Ll

Mm

Ww

Ll

Ff

Pp

Bb

Ff

Pp

Mm

Ff

Pp

Pp

Ff

Pp

Name _____

Beginning Sounds

Draw one picture for each letter.

b	**s**
w	**m**
h	**p**

Listen for the Sound

Skill: Listening for Initial Consonant Sounds: *c, d, j, q, n, v*

Preparing the Center

1. Prepare an envelope following the directions on page 3.
    Cover—page 111
    Student Directions—page 113
    Sorting Pockets—pages 115–119
    Task Cards—pages 121 and 123
2. Reproduce a supply of the student activity sheet on page 125.
3. Place all center materials in the envelope.

Using the Center

In a Small Group

Lay the sorting pockets on a flat surface. Students choose a card and say the name of the picture, listening for the beginning sound. They place the card in the toy box with the letter that matches that sound.

Independently

The student places the blocks in the toy box according to the beginning sounds.

The student then matches pictures with the same beginning sound on the activity sheet.

Self-Checking Key

Turn over each set of task cards. The letter on the back of each should be the same as the letter on the toy box.

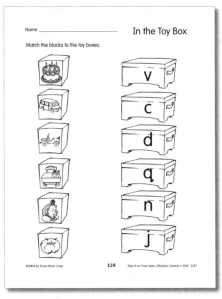

Listen for the Sound

Listen for the Sound

1. Read the letters on the toy boxes.

2. Choose each toy block. Say the name of the picture.

3. Listen for the beginning sound. Match it to a toy box.

4. Turn over the blocks to check your answers.

5. Do the activity sheet.

Skill: Listening for Initial Consonants: *c, d, j, q, n, v*

114

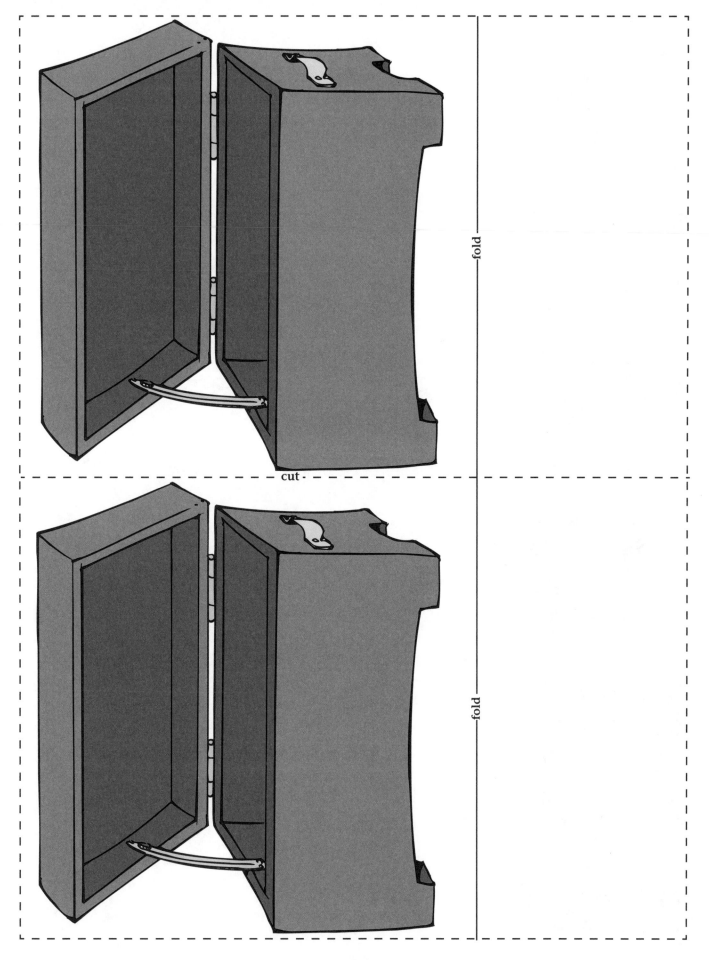

cut

fold

fold

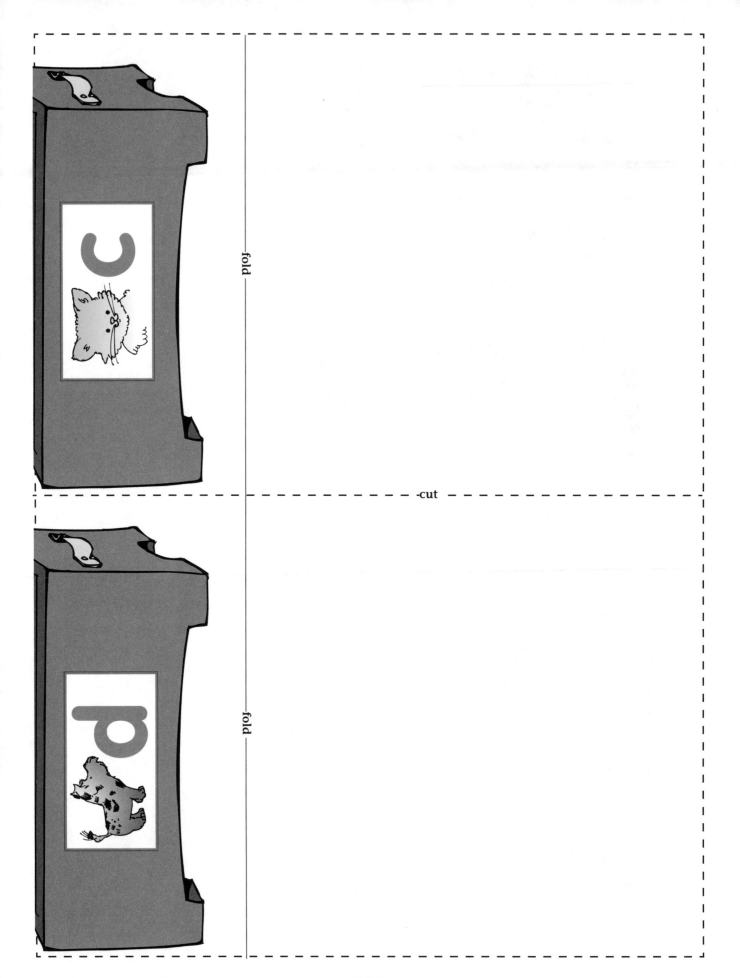

fold

fold

-cut

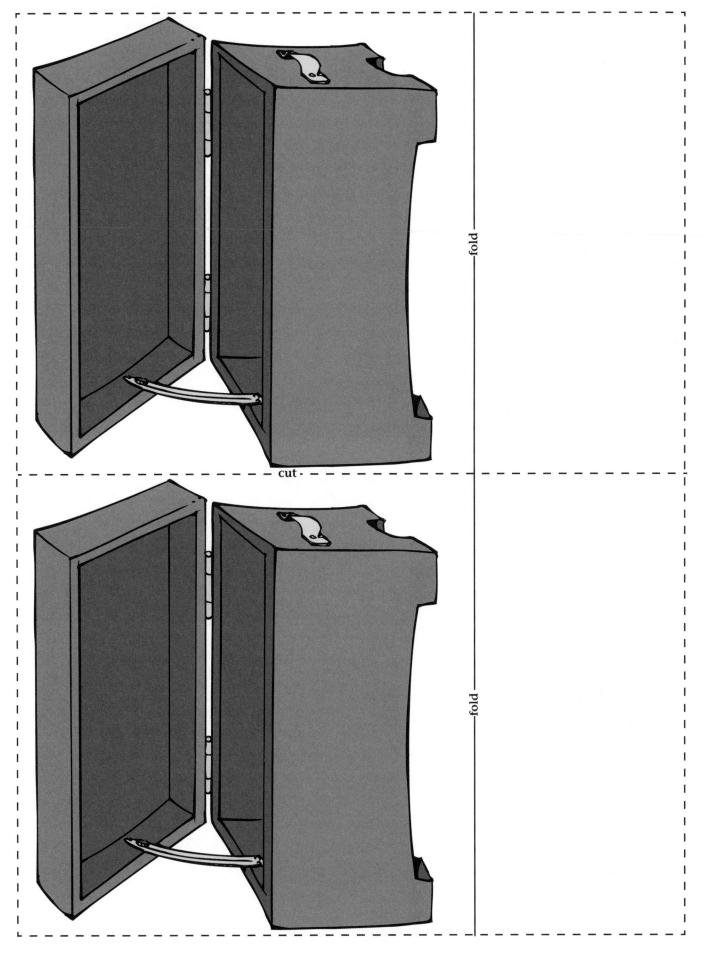

cut

fold

fold

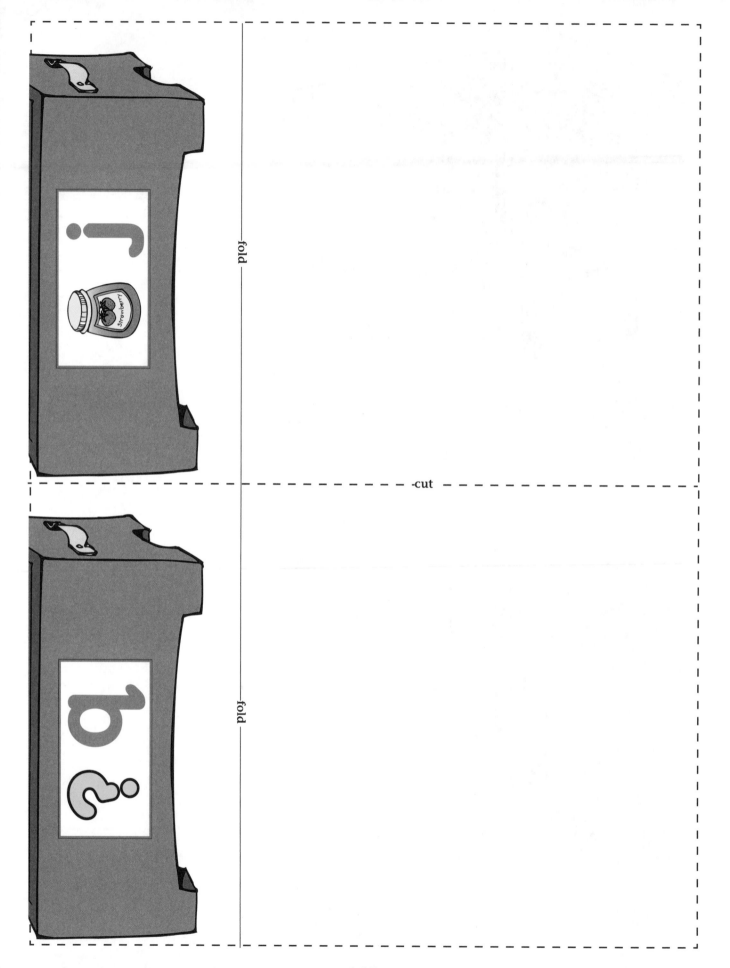

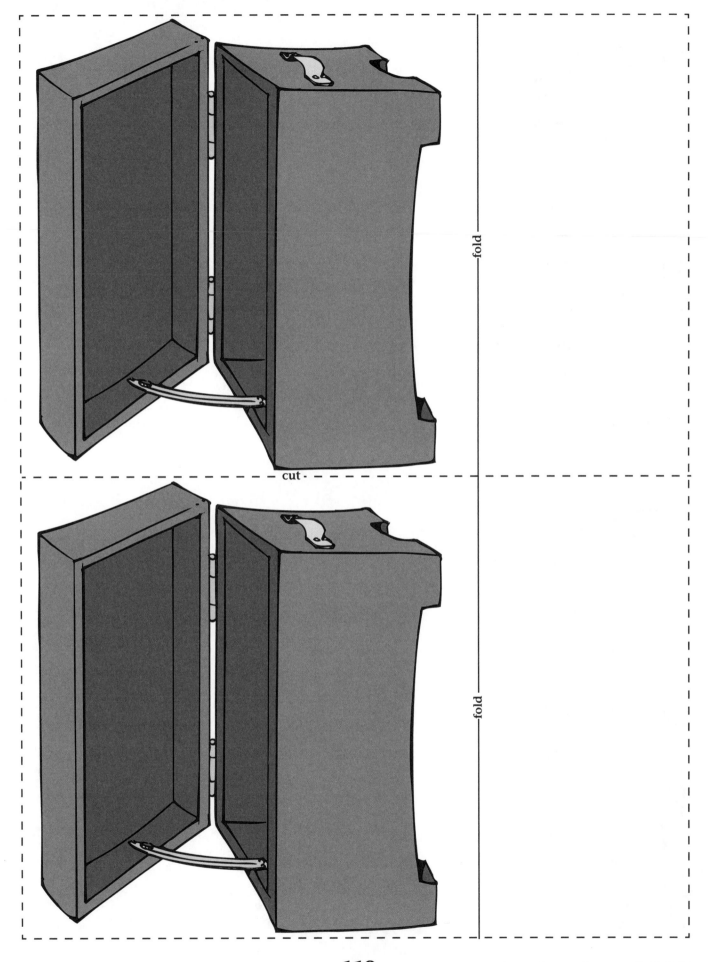

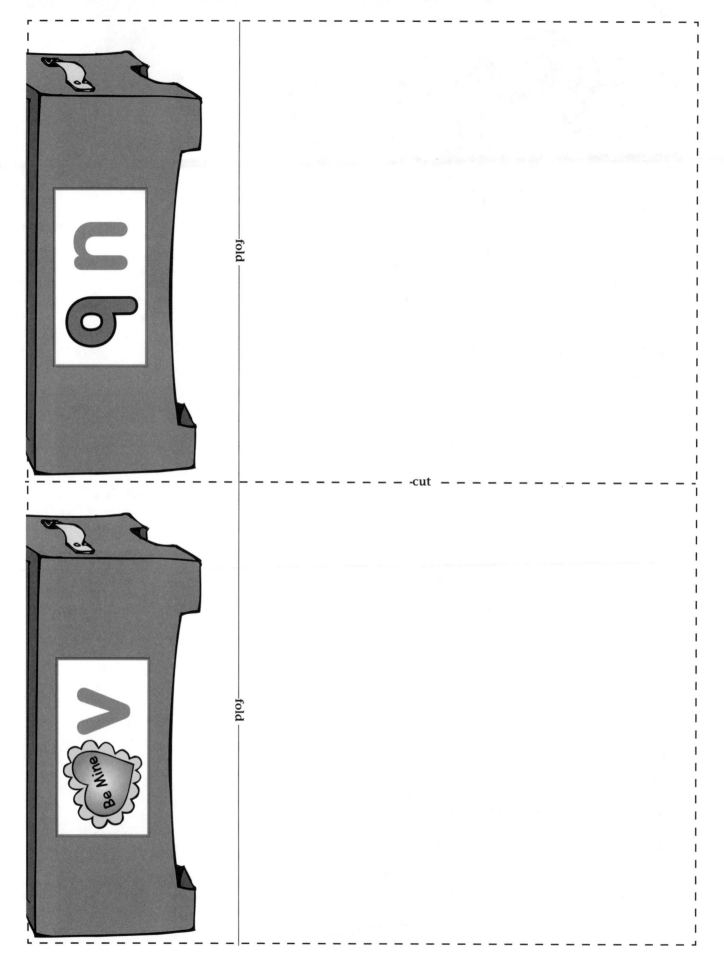

j

c

d

j

c

d

j

c

d

j

c

d

v

n

q

v

n

q

v

n

q

v

n

q

Name _____

Match the blocks to the toy boxes.

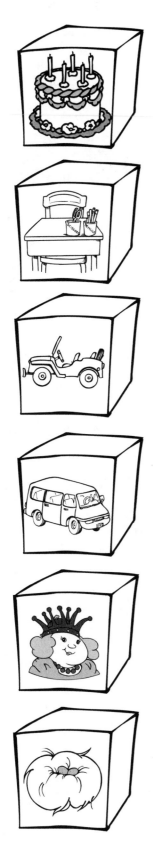

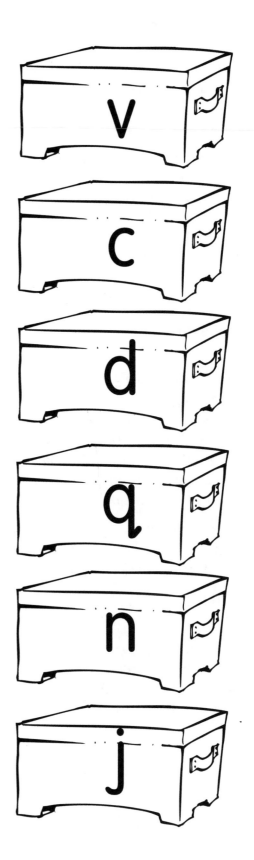

Begins With...

Skill: Listening for Initial Consonant Sounds: *g, k, r, t, y, z*

Preparing the Center

1. Prepare an envelope following the directions on page 3.
   - Cover—page 127
   - Student Directions—page 129
   - Sorting Mats—pages 131 and 133
   - Task Cards—pages 135 and 137
2. Reproduce a supply of the student activity sheet on page 139.
3. Place all center materials in the envelope.

Using the Center

In a Small Group

Students choose a task card and say the name of the picture, listening for the beginning sound. They place the picture in the column on the sorting mat that names the beginning sound.

Independently

The student sorts and places the task cards on the correct mats.

On the activity sheet, the student draws one picture for each letter.

Self-Checking Key

Turn over each set of three task cards. The letter on the back of each card should match the letter on the sorting mat.

Begins With...

Begins With...

1. Read the letters on the sorting mats.

2. Choose each card. Say the name of the picture.

3. Listen for the beginning sound. Match it to a sorting mat.

4. Turn over the cards to check your answers.

5. Do the activity sheet.

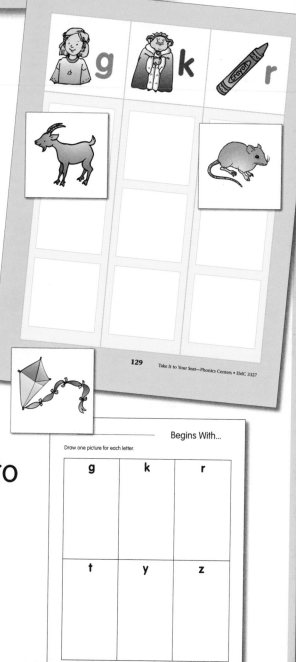

Skill: Listening for Initial Consonants: *g, k, r, t, y, z*

130

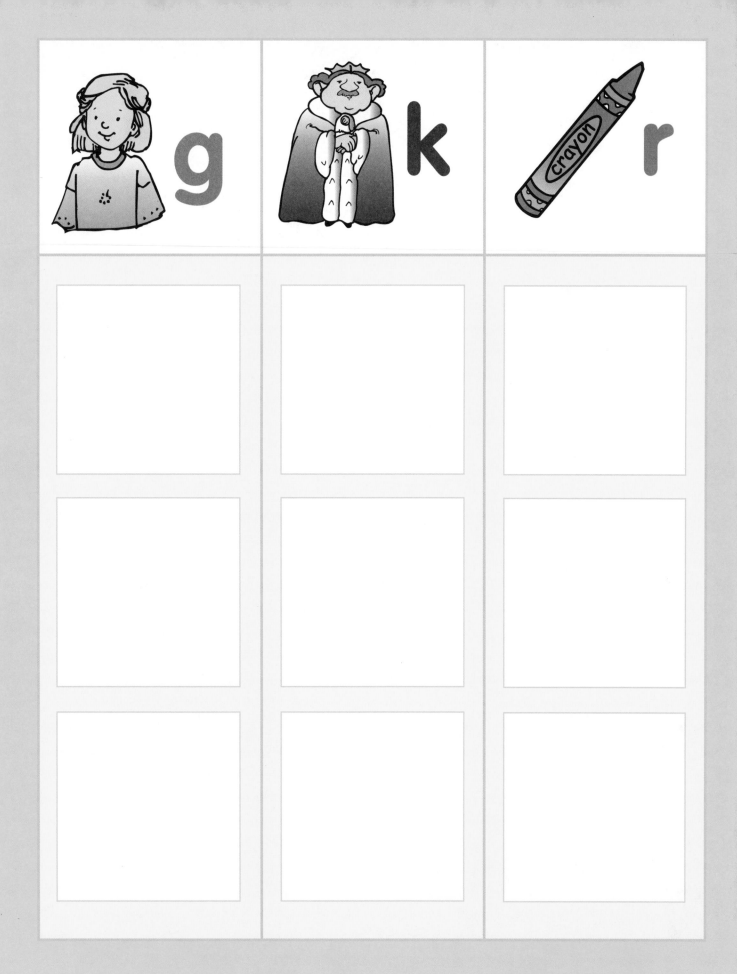

g   k   r

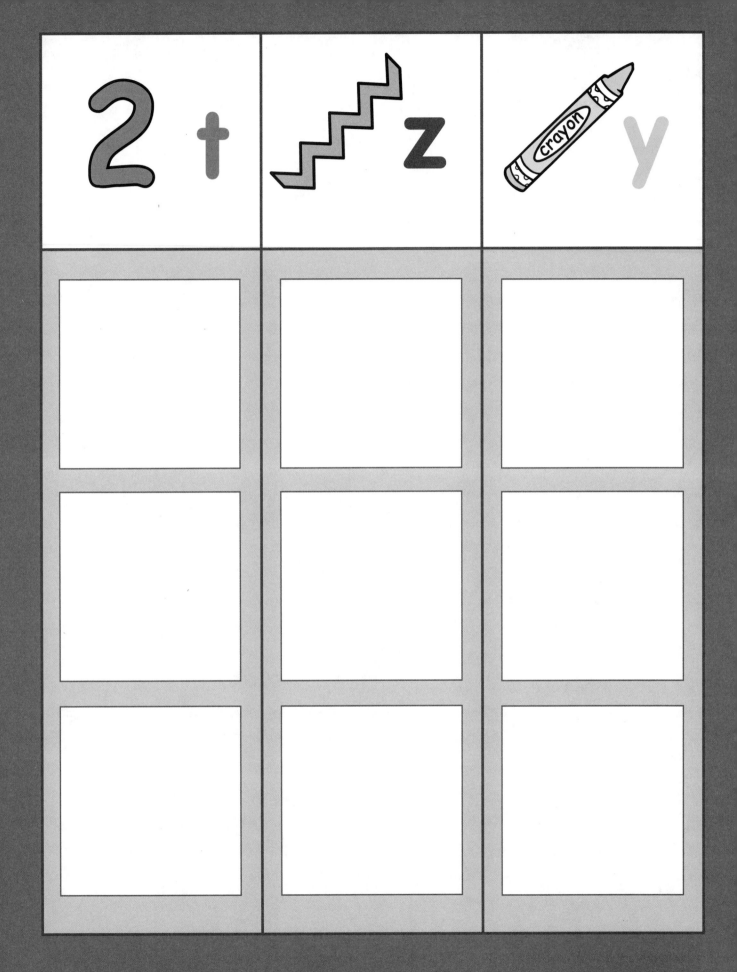

134

r

k

g

r

k

g

r

k

g

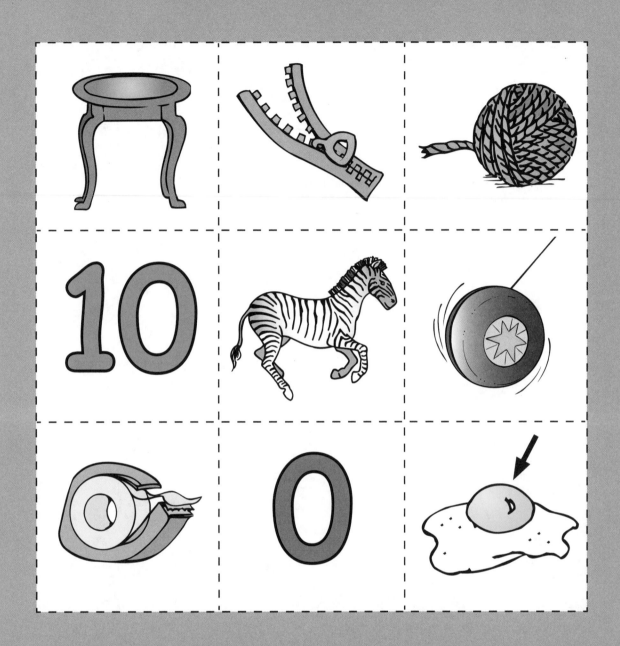

y

z

t

y

z

t

y

z

t

Name _____

Begins With...

Draw one picture for each letter.

g	k	r
t	**y**	**z**

Ending Sounds

Skill: Listening for Final Consonant Sounds: *b, k, n, s, t*

Preparing the Center

1. Prepare an envelope following the directions on page 3.
   - Cover—page 141
   - Student Directions—page 143
   - Task Cards—pages 145–153
2. Reproduce a supply of the student activity sheet on page 155.
3. Place all center materials in the envelope.

Using the Center

In a Small Group

Lay the letter cards and picture cards faceup on a flat surface. Hold up a letter card. Students find pictures whose names end with the letter on the card. Students name each of the pictures, listen for the sound of the letter, and then place the pictures around the correct letter card. The pictures with the same ending sound form a square with the letter in the center.

Independently

The student lays the letter cards faceup on a flat surface. The student selects a picture card and names the picture. The student places the card beside the letter that stands for the sound that is heard at the end of the word. The four picture cards are to be placed to form a square with the letter in the center.

Then the student matches pictures with the correct ending sound on the student activity sheet.

Self-Checking Key

Students turn the cards over to make sure the designs on the back match.

Ending Sounds

b

142

Ending Sounds

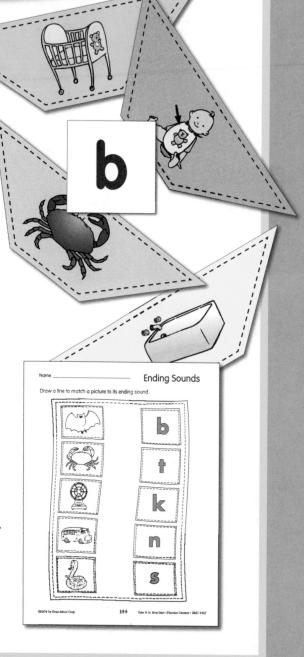

1. Read the letters.

2. Choose each picture. Say the name. Listen for the ending sound.

3. Match each picture to the letter you hear at the end of the word.

4. Make the shapes into squares.

5. Turn over the squares to check your answers.

6. Do the activity sheet.

Skill: Listening for Final Consonant Sounds: *b, k, n, s, t*

144

Cut the quilt pieces apart on the solid lines.

 Take It to Your Seat—Phonics Centers • EMC 3327

146

Cut the quilt pieces apart on the solid lines.

147

Cut the quilt pieces apart on the solid lines.

Take It to Your Seat—Phonics Centers • EMC 3327

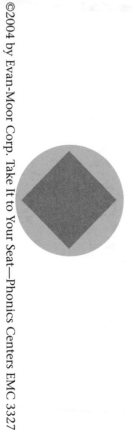

Cut the quilt pieces apart on the solid lines.

151 Take It to Your Seat—Phonics Centers • EMC 3327

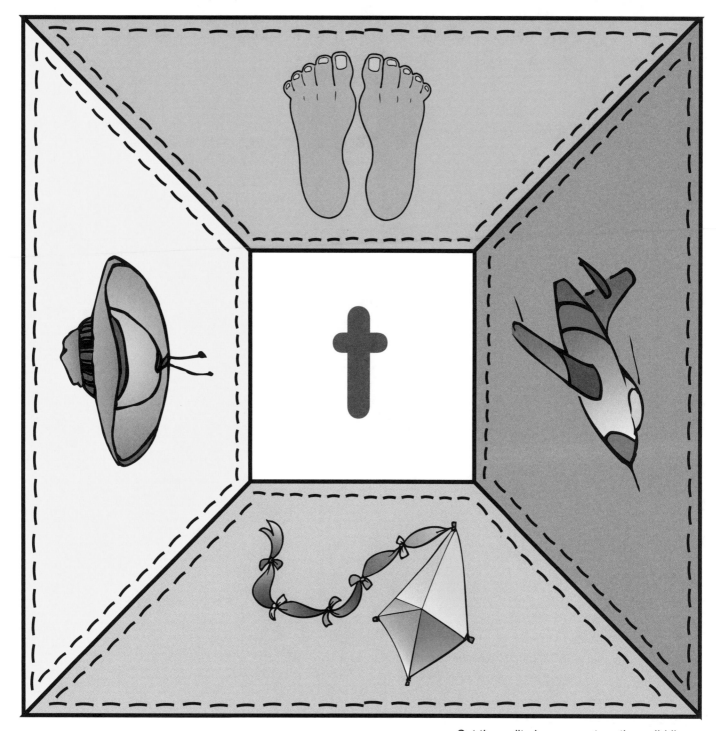

Cut the quilt pieces apart on the solid lines.

Name _____

Ending Sounds

Draw a line to match each picture to its ending sound.

Ends With...

Skill: Listening for Final Consonant
Sounds: *d, g, l, m, p, r*

Preparing the Center

1. Prepare an envelope following the directions on page 3.
   - Cover—page 157
   - Student Directions—page 159
   - Task Cards—
     - Letter cones—pages 161 and 163
     - Ice-cream scoops—pages 165–169
2. Reproduce a supply of the student activity sheet on page 171.
3. Place all center materials in the envelope.

Using the Center

In a Small Group

Lay the cones containing letters and the ice-cream scoops containing pictures faceup on a flat surface. Hold up a letter cone. Students find pictures whose names end with the letter on the cone. Students name each of the pictures, listen for the sound of the letter, and then place the ice-cream scoops on the cone.

Independently

The student lays the cones and ice-cream scoops faceup on a flat surface. The student selects an ice-cream scoop and names the picture. The student places the scoop on the cone whose letter stands for the sound that is heard at the end of the picture name.

Then the student matches pictures with the sound heard at the end of each word on the student activity sheet.

Self-Checking Key

Turn over the three scoops in each ice-cream cone. Matching pieces will have the same letter on the back as the cone.

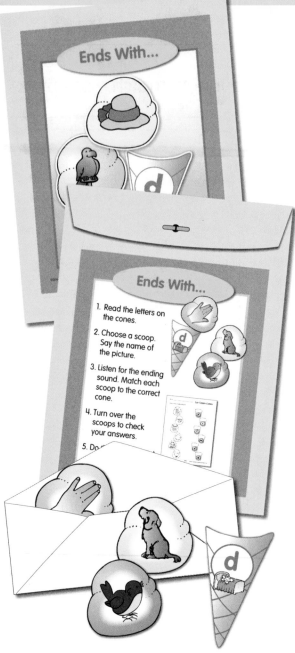

Ends With...

158

Ends With...

1. Read the letters on the cones.

2. Choose a scoop. Say the name of the picture.

3. Listen for the ending sound. Match each scoop to the correct cone.

4. Turn over the scoops to check your answers.

5. Do the activity sheet.

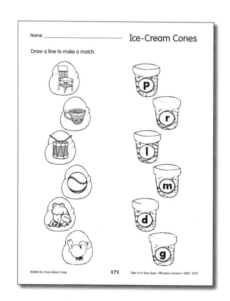

Skill: Listening for Final Consonant Sounds: *d, g, l, m, p, r*

Take It to Your Seat—Phonics Centers • EMC 3327

160

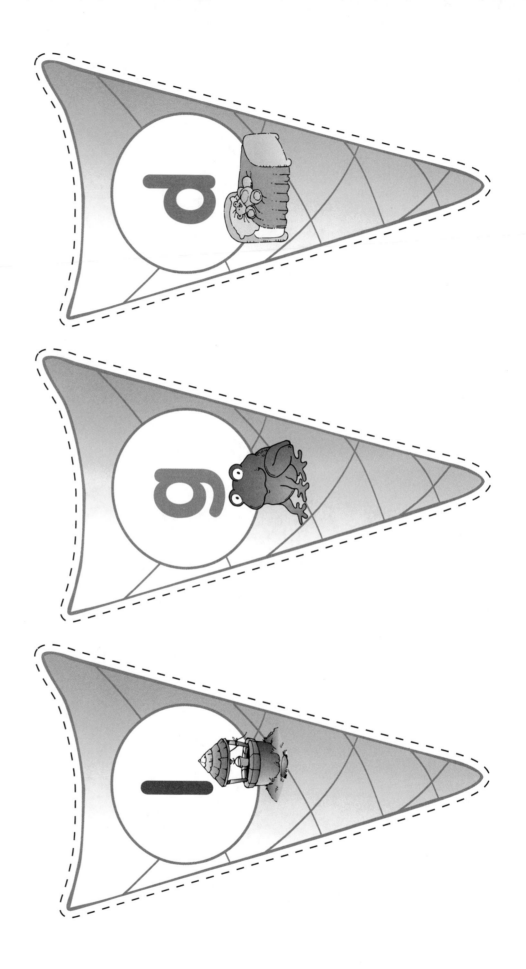

©2004 by Evan-Moor Corp.
Take It to Your Seat—
Phonics Centers
EMC 3327

©2004 by Evan-Moor Corp.
Take It to Your Seat—
Phonics Centers
EMC 3327

©2004 by Evan-Moor Corp.
Take It to Your Seat—
Phonics Centers
EMC 3327

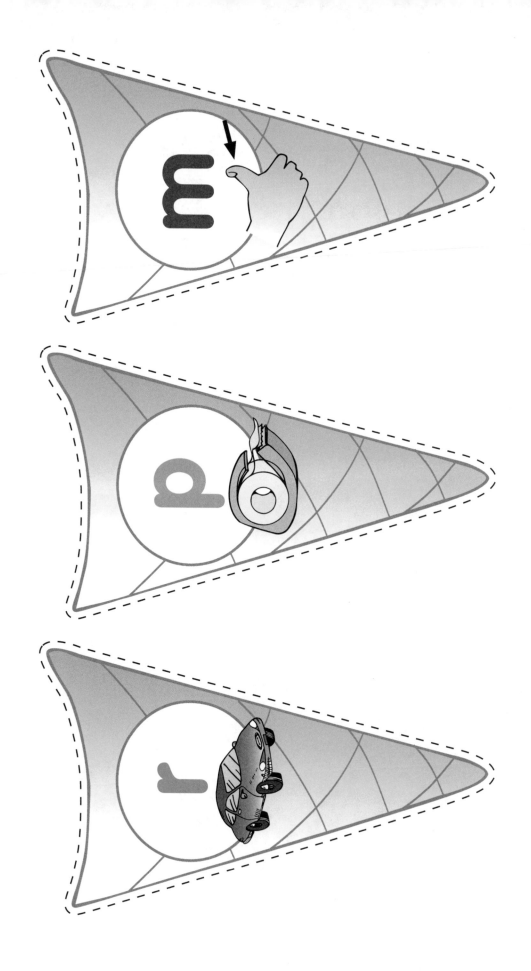

Ice-Cream Cones

Draw a line to make a match.

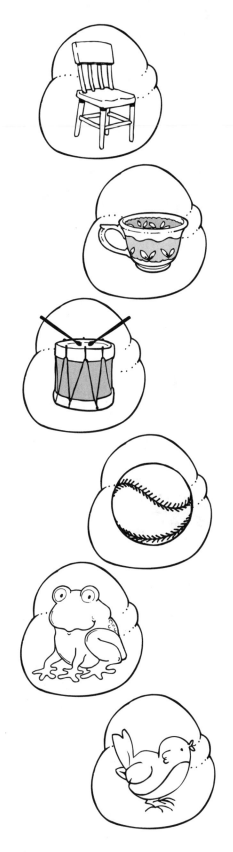

Count the Parts

Skill: Counting Syllables

Preparing the Center

1. Prepare an envelope following the directions on page 3.
   - Cover—page 173
   - Student Directions—page 175
   - Sorting Pockets—pages 177 and 179
   - Task Cards—pages 181–189
2. Reproduce a supply of the activity sheet on page 191.
3. Place all center materials in the envelope.

Using the Center

In a Small Group

Give each student a sorting pocket. Place the task cards in a small bag or box. One at a time, students draw a card and name the picture. The group decides how many parts the word contains. The student who drew the card places the picture in the correct sorting pocket. Students take turns drawing cards until the bag or box is empty.

Independently

The student sorts the cards by number of syllables, placing each picture in the correct sorting pocket.

On the activity sheet, the student names each picture and circles the number of parts it contains.

Self-Checking Key

Turn over the picture cards and read the number on the back.

Count the Parts

cluck

I hear 1

ribbit

I hear 2

174

Count the Parts

1. Take the pockets.

2. Choose a card. Say the name of the picture on the card.

3. Did you hear 1 part or 2 parts? Put the card in the correct pocket.

4. Put all the cards in the correct pockets.

5. Do the activity sheet.

Skill: Counting Syllables

176

fold

fold

Count the Parts

fold

Count the Parts

1

1

1

1

1

1

1

1

2

2

2

2

2

2

2

2

1

1

1

1

1

1

1

1

1

1

1

1

2

2

2

2

2

©2004 by Evan-Moor Corp.
Take It to Your Seat—Phonics Centers
EMC 3327

2

©2004 by Evan-Moor Corp.
Take It to Your Seat—Phonics Centers
EMC 3327

2

©2004 by Evan-Moor Corp.
Take It to Your Seat—Phonics Centers
EMC 3327

2

©2004 by Evan-Moor Corp.
Take It to Your Seat—Phonics Centers
EMC 3327

2

©2004 by Evan-Moor Corp.
Take It to Your Seat—Phonics Centers
EMC 3327

2

©2004 by Evan-Moor Corp.
Take It to Your Seat—Phonics Centers
EMC 3327

2

©2004 by Evan-Moor Corp.
Take It to Your Seat—Phonics Centers
EMC 3327

2

©2004 by Evan-Moor Corp.
Take It to Your Seat—Phonics Centers
EMC 3327

Name _____

Count the Parts

Name the picture. Circle the number of parts.

1　　**2**	**1**　　**2**	**1**　　**2**
1　　**2**	**1**　　**2**	**1**　　**2**
1　　**2**	**1**　　**2**	**1**　　**2**

Answer Key

Page 13
Puppy Match

Draw a line to match.

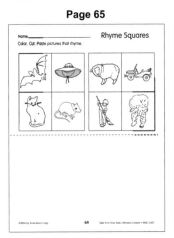

Page 27
Find the Pairs

Color the two letters in each row that are the same.

1. (a) b (a) 7. (g) (g) p
2. (c) (c) s 8. c (e) (e)
3. (f) x (f) 9. (h) n (h)
4. (j) f (j) 10. (j) g (j)
5. (w) (w) x 11. h (k) (k)
6. d (a) (a) 12. (m) (m) n

Page 41
Three of a Kind

Circle the 3 that are the same.

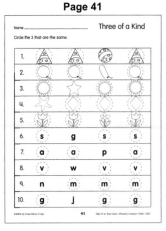

6. (s) g (s) (s)
7. (a) (a) p (a)
8. (v) w (v) (v)
9. n (m) (m) (m)
10. (g) j (g) (g)

Page 53
Rhyming Pairs

Draw a line to show the rhyme.

Page 65
Rhyme Squares

Color. Cut. Paste pictures that rhyme.

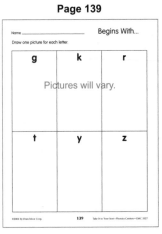

Page 77
Alike–Not Alike

Color the correct face.

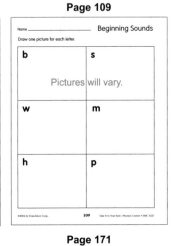

Page 109
Beginning Sounds

Draw one picture for each letter.

b	s
Pictures will vary.	
w	m
h	p

Page 125
In the Toy Box

Match the blocks to the toy boxes.

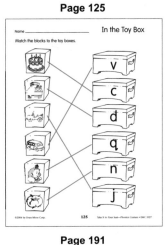

Page 139
Begins With...

Draw one picture for each letter.

g	k	r
Pictures will vary.		
t	y	z

Page 155
Ending Sounds

Draw a line to match each picture to its ending sound.

Page 171
Ice-Cream Cones

Draw a line to make a match.

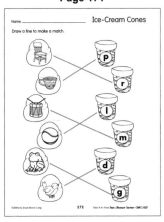

Page 191
Count the Parts

Name the picture. Circle the number of parts.

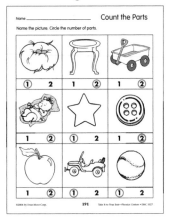